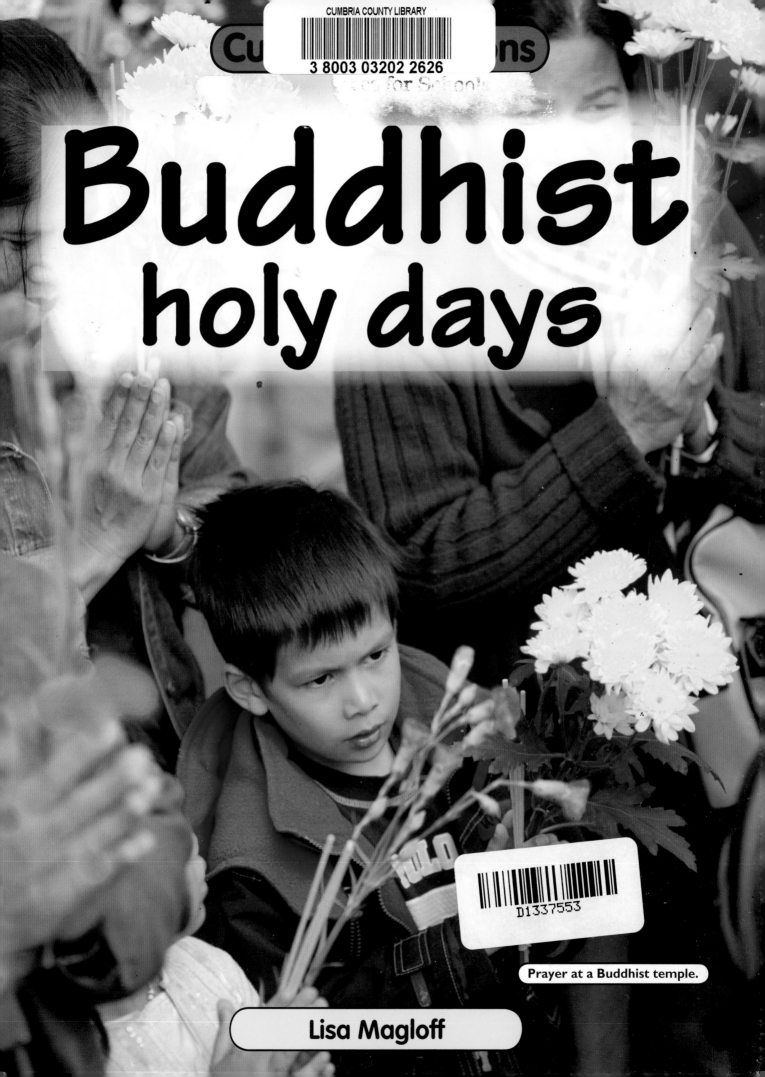

Buddhist
holy days

Prayer at a Buddhist temple.

Lisa Magloff

Glossary

ALMS Donations of food and other items made to monks and nuns.

ARAHANT A person who has become enlightened. It is a name given to the Buddha and to the highest level of his followers.

BUDDHA The Enlightened or Awakened One. The founder of Buddhism. The word comes from 'Bodhi', which means 'to awaken'.

BUDDHISM The name of the religion of people who follow the teachings of the Buddha.

DHAMMA The teachings of the Buddha.

ENLIGHTENMENT The goal of Buddhism. When someone is enlightened, they understand the truth of life, and are free from all ignorance and fear.

FIVE PRECEPTS The five rules of conduct given by the Buddha to his disciples: no killing, no stealing, no sexual misconduct, no false speech (no lying or telling tales), and no intoxicants (drugs and alcohol).

FOUR NOBLE TRUTHS The first teachings spoken by the Buddha. They are the truth of: suffering exists; we are the cause of our own suffering; it is possible to end our suffering; Buddhism can show us the way to end our suffering.

HOLY PEOPLE In ancient India there were many people who travelled around, living simply and without possessions, and preaching. Ordinary people believe that these holy men were closer to enlightenment than others.

MEDITATE/MEDITATION A method of calming and training the mind by sitting quietly and concentrating.

MONASTERY A large temple, usually with many monks or nuns in residence. Monasteries may be made up of many buildings, including temples and schools.

MONK A man who has given up everything and decided to devote his life to Buddhism.

NOVICE A monk or nun in training, or a person who is living as a monk or nun only temporarily.

NUN A woman who has given up everything and decided to devote her life to Buddhism.

OFFERINGS A way of showing respect and devotion to the Buddha, or to monks and nuns, by giving gifts with special meanings. Offerings can be very simple, such as water, flowers or fruit.

RAINY SEASON In some parts of the world, such as the places where Buddhism began, most of the rain falls at one time of year. At this time it rains very heavily and farmers cannot work in the fields. In ancient times, when there was little irrigation, the rains that fell during this season would also determine how good the harvests would be. So, this was a time of rest and also a time to find out if there would be enough food in the coming seasons.

SANGHA The worldwide community of Buddhist nuns and monks.

SERMON A talk or teaching given by a learned or holy person.

TEMPLE A place where Buddhists go to learn about Buddhism, to talk with monks or nuns and to practise rituals of devotion, such as leaving offerings or chanting prayers.

Contents

As you go through the book, look for words in **BOLD CAPITALS**. These words are defined in the glossary.

⚠ Understanding others

Remember that other people's beliefs are important to them. You must always be considerate and understanding when studying about faith.

Offerings at a Buddhist temple in London.

What is a holy day?

There are many different types of Buddhist holiday.

People of all faiths worship throughout the whole year. But in all faiths, some days are special. These special days, or holy days, may remember an important event in the history of the faith, or they may be written about in holy writings, or scripture.

These holy days are different from a day of rest and worship that many religions have each week. Many holy days involve public celebrations, special meals, festivals and even processions. In general, we call these special days holy days and it is from this that we get the word 'holiday'.

Whereas Muslims reserve Friday as a special day, Jews Saturday and Christians Sunday, Buddhists have no special weekly day of rest. Many Buddhists worship at home every day and go to the temple to worship one or more times each week.

▼ Worshippers carry offerings of flowers to a Buddhist temple.

But there are also many holy days and times throughout the year, each with their own name. Many of these days and times celebrate or remember important events in the life of the **BUDDHA**, the founder of the Buddhist faith. Other holy days remember the teachings of the Buddha.

Different holy days

All Buddhists believe in the Buddha and in the importance of the Buddha's teachings. But there are many different traditions in **BUDDHISM**. Some Buddhist holidays are celebrated only by Buddhists from a particular tradition. For example, each August, Buddhists in Kandy, Sri Lanka, celebrate a holy day called the Festival of the Tooth, where one of the Buddha's teeth is displayed to the public. This holiday is not celebrated by any other Buddhists. Other holidays are celebrated by Buddhists all over the world.

The way a holiday is celebrated may also change from place to place. As you look at the main holy days of the Buddhist faith in this book, notice how there are many different ways to mark out or celebrate each day.

The Buddhist holy day calendar

Here are the parts of the year when Buddhist holidays occur.

To keep track of the days of the year, many people in the world use a calendar which divides the year into 12 months and begins on January 1. In this calendar, the Sun is used as a guide and one year is about the time it takes the Earth to move around the Sun.

But not all calendars look like this. Some calendars, for example, use the way the Moon moves across the sky as a guide. So, the holy days change dates a little each year. This is how the Buddhist calendars work. But because there are many different Buddhist traditions, there are also many different Buddhist calendars. So some of the holidays occur on different dates in different countries. In general, each month begins on the New Moon and ends when the next New Moon is sighted.

Buddhism began in India and spread first to southeast Asia. In these places, there is a RAINY SEASON each year. In ancient times, when Buddhism began, the rain was important for growing crops, but it was also difficult for farmers and other people to do work during the rainy season. So, many Buddhist holidays also have to do with celebrating the beginning or end of the rainy season.

Buddhist months

In many Buddhist traditions the months are not named, but are only numbered. Below is an example of a Buddhist calendar based on the phases of the Moon.

Buddhist Calendar	
1st Month	Dec/Jan
2nd Month	Jan/Feb
3rd Month	Feb/Mar
4th Month	Mar/Apr
5th Month	Apr/May
6th Month	May/Jun
7th Month	Jun/Jul
8th Month	Jul/Aug
9th Month	Aug/Sep
10th Month	Sep/Oct
11th Month	Oct/Nov
12th Month	Nov/Dec
A 13th Month is added every few years as a leap month.	

▶ In this chart, you can see how the Buddhist holy days are spread around the year. You can also see how some of the holidays (based on the Moon) move around a little from year to year.

BUDDHIST HOLY DAYS

	2007	**2008**	**2009**	**2010**	**2011**
Losar begins	Feb 18	Feb 8	Feb 26	Feb 16	Feb 4
Magha Puja	Dates vary, usually in March				
Songkran	In Thailand it is always April 13–15				
Vesak	May 2	May 20	May 9	May 27	May 17
Dhamma Day	June 30	July 18	July 7	June 26	July 15
Kathina	Varies from monastery to monastery				
Ancestor Day	June 30	July 18	July 7	June 26	July 15
Ullambana and O-bon are always July 13					
Dates are approximate and may vary from country to country					

The New Year

Buddhists celebrate the New Year as a time to think about making a new beginning.

Because there are many different Buddhist calendars, there are also many different Buddhist New Years. For example, Buddhists from Thailand, Burma, Sri Lanka, Cambodia and Laos celebrate New Year's Day on the first day of the Full Moon in April. But in China, Korea and Vietnam, Buddhist New Year is celebrated in mid-January.

Whenever New Year is celebrated, it is always a happy and joyous time. Here are some different ways that Buddhist New Year is celebrated.

The Tibetan New Year

In early February Tibetan Buddhists celebrate their New Year holiday, called Losar. In Tibet, this is one of the most important holidays of the year. Losar lasts for three or more days.

Losar is a time to welcome in a new beginning, so most people get ready by cleaning their houses and other buildings inside and outside, and buy new clothes to wear. The **MONKS** and **NUNS** clean and decorate the **MONASTERIES** and **TEMPLES**.

▼ The monkey temple, near Kathmandu, Nepal, is decorated with prayer flags to celebrate the Tibetan New Year. The coloured flags have prayers written on them.

On the first day of the holiday, everyone gets up very early and goes to the temple or monastery to offer prayers to make up for any mistakes made during the past year and to hope for a good year. **OFFERINGS** of food and other gifts are left for the monks and nuns, and candles and incense are lit in front of statues of the Buddha. People greet each other by saying "tashi delek", which means 'good luck'.

On the second and third days of the holiday, people visit friends and family, exchange gifts and share festive meals. One food eaten during Losar is a type of sweet called kapsey.

One Losar tradition is to make cooked dough balls with ingredients such as chillies, salt, wool, rice and even coal hidden inside. These are then given to friends. If a person finds a chilli in their dough ball, it means they will be very talkative in the New Year. If a person finds wood or coal inside, they will have a happy year.

The Thai New Year

For Thai Buddhists, the New Year holiday is called Songkran and is celebrated on April 13 to 15.

Many people start the holiday by cleaning their houses and other buildings. One tradition is that anything old or useless must be thrown away at this time of year, or it will bring bad luck to its owner.

On the first day of the holiday, people go to temples to worship and to make offerings to the monks and nuns. Worshippers pour bowls of water on to statues of the Buddha.

▼ On New Year's Day, Thai Buddhists may give monks and nuns offerings of practical things they need for everyday life.

▶ Pouring water into the hands of relatives and elders is a type of offering and a way to show respect.

This is one way of thanking the Buddha for his teachings. Statues of the Buddha are also carried through the streets in processions, and people pour water on them as they pass by.

In Thailand, this is the hottest time of the year and so one very popular tradition during the New Year's holiday is to throw water on people. In Thailand this holiday is sometimes called the 'water festival'.

During this holiday, young people visit their older relatives. The young people pour scented water into the hands of their parents and older relatives. This is a way to show them respect. After this, elder members of the family offer their blessings for a good New Year. Families may then go to a temple to worship and then have a festive meal together.

Another tradition is to carry handfuls of sand or earth to the temple. This is to replace the dirt that people carry away on their feet during the rest of the year. The sand is then piled into large sand castles and decorated with colourful flags.

Magha Puja Day

This holiday takes place on the Full Moon in March.

The holy day of Magha Puja is also called Sangha Day and Fourfold Assembly Day. Magha Puja takes place on the Full Moon in the third month of the Buddhist year (February or March) and celebrates an important event in the life of the Buddha.

The story of Magha Puja

After the Buddha began teaching, many of the people who heard his **SERMONS** decided to become his disciples, or followers. These people spent their time travelling around India studying and teaching others about Buddhism. Many of these **HOLY PEOPLE** soon became very wise from their study of Buddhism. These especially wise and holy Buddhists were called **ARAHANTS**.

One year, in the third month, the Buddha decided to go to the Veluwan Temple in the city of Rajaha, India. When he got to the temple, the Buddha was met by 1,250 arahants. All of these people had come to the temple from all over India on the same day, without being asked and without arranging it with each other first. They simply showed up at the same time as the Buddha.

At the temple, the Buddha gave a talk where he set out the basic rules and guidelines for the monks and nuns. This was the beginning of the **SANGHA**, the worldwide community of Buddhist monks and nuns.

▲▶ Magha Puja prayers on the steps of a Buddhist temple. People are holding flowers as offerings to the Buddha.

This holiday is sometimes called the Fourfold Assembly. The name comes from the fact that four important things happened on this day: 1,250 people gathered (assembled) at the Veluwan Temple on the same day without being asked; all of the 1,250 people were arahants; all of the people who gathered had been taught by the Buddha; and it was the Full Moon.

13

Celebrating Magha Puja

Magha Puja is a time for celebrating Buddhism and the worldwide community of Buddhist monks and nuns. This is also a time when Buddhists renew their commitment to the ideals of Buddhism and to the Buddhist way of life.

All over the world, many people go to the temple on this day to worship, **MEDITATE**, chant prayers, read from holy scriptures and listen to talks about Buddhism.

▼▶ Lighting incense as an offering at a temple.

People may also light candles and incense and give offerings of food and other things to the monks and nuns. There may be candle lit processions at temples at night.

This is also a time for Buddhists to socialise with each other. People gather with friends for festive meals and exchange small gifts. Many temples also organise dinners where worshippers can meet and discuss their faith as well as socialise.

▲ There are often special worship services on Magha Puja day.

▶ Many people bring offerings of food for the monks and nuns, or cook meals at the temple to share with the entire community.

Vesak

This is the most important holy day of the Buddhist year.

The holiday of Vesak, or Buddha Day is celebrated by Buddhists all over the world. For most Buddhists, it takes place on the Full Moon in the sixth month of the Buddhist year (May/June).

Vesak remembers three events: the Buddha's birthday, the day he became **ENLIGHTENED** and the day he died. All of these things happened on the same day in different years.

The story of the Buddha

The Buddha was born Siddhartha Gautama around 566 BCE in India. His father was a king and his mother was queen. As he grew up, Siddhartha began to wonder why people suffer in life. Finally, when he was 29, Siddhartha left his family and his luxurious life in the palace and became a wandering monk.

Siddhartha travelled for many years, searching for a way to end suffering. He studied with many different holy men and tried many different ways to find peace, but nothing worked.

After six years of studying and wandering, Siddhartha sat down to meditate under a tree at Bodh Gaya, in north-eastern India. After three days and nights, Siddhartha realised what causes people to suffer and how to stop it. He had become enlightened. After this, Siddhartha Gautama was called the Buddha, which means 'the awakened one', or 'the enlightened one'.

For the next 45 years, the Buddha taught people how they could be free from suffering and become enlightened.

The Buddha died in around 486 BCE at the age of 80. Buddhist tradition says that the Buddha decided exactly when to die and ate some poisoned food. He then lay on his side and meditated until he died.

▼ In Korea, Vesak is often celebrated by carrying colourful paper lanterns in processions. The lights are a reminder of the light of Buddha's teachings.

Celebrating Vesak

There are many different ways to celebrate Vesak. But all of them have to do with remembering the Buddha and his teachings, and with thanking the Buddha.

In many places, people go to their local temple in the days before Vesak and help clean it and decorate it with lights and lanterns.

They may also clean and decorate their homes.

On the night before Vesak, monks and nuns may stay up all night, chanting prayers and meditating. In the morning, worshippers go to the temples. They make offerings of incense, flowers, candles, water and prayers for the Buddha. They also leave offerings of food and robes for the monks and nuns.

◄▼ Candles and other types of light are popular temple offerings on Vesak.

The 'Bathing of the Buddha' is another Vesak tradition. Worshippers pour water over a statue of the Buddha as a reminder that the Buddha taught his followers how to make their minds and hearts clean and pure.

Many people stay at the temple all day to chant prayers, meditate and think about the Buddha.

▼ Bathing the Buddha is one way that worshippers show they will try to keep their thoughts pure.

There may also be talks and lectures about the Buddha's life and teachings. After worship there may be festive meals and candle lit processions through the streets or in monasteries.

Different traditions

Each Buddhist country has different traditions for how to celebrate Vesak.

In China, processions include large paper dragons. In Indonesia, Vesak lanterns are made from paper and wood and placed in homes, temples and other buildings.

Another popular tradition in some countries is to buy and release caged birds. The birds are a reminder of the Buddha's teaching that all living things should be free and happy.

Buddhists in Japan make paper cranes that are floated down rivers. These are a reminder of the Buddha's teaching that we should let go of our problems and not spend all of our time thinking about them.

▲ Japanese paper cranes.

▲ A statue of the Buddha. His hands are in the position called Dhammachakra, which means 'Wheel of Dhamma'. Dhamma are the Buddha's teachings and this statue is a reminder of the Buddha's first sermon. The outstretched fingers of the right hand stand for the people who listen to the teachings. The hands are held in front of the heart, which shows that these teachings come straight from the Buddha's heart.

Dhamma Day and the Rains Retreat

This holiday celebrates the Buddha's first teaching.

Dhamma Day is celebrated on the Full Moon of the eighth month (usually July/August), on the Buddhist calendar. In some places, this holiday is also called Ashala Puja. It celebrates the beginning of the Buddhist faith and the first teaching that the Buddha gave after he became enlightened.

The Buddha's first teaching

After the Buddha became enlightened he travelled to a deer park in the city of Sarnath, which is near Benares, India. In the deer park, the Buddha met with five of his friends. These five people were also looking for a way to end suffering, and the Buddha told them what he had learned. This was the Buddha's first teaching, or sermon.

In this sermon, the Buddha told his friends the **FOUR NOBLE TRUTHS**. These are the basis of the Buddhist faith. The Four Noble Truths are: everyone has suffering in their lives; there are reasons why suffering happens; it is possible to

Weblink: www.CurriculumVisions.com

end suffering; everyone can become enlightened.

This first teaching is also called 'The First Turning of the Wheel of Truth'. The word DHAMMA means truth, and the teachings of the Buddha are sometimes called the path of dhamma, or the path of truth.

After the Buddha gave his sermon, his five friends decided to become followers, or disciples, of the Buddha. These five people became the first Buddhist monks. So, this day is the beginning of the Buddhist faith and also the beginning of Buddhist monks and nuns.

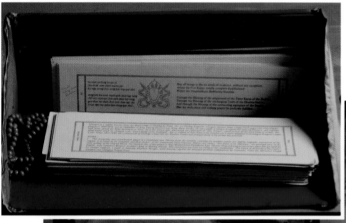

▲ In some traditions, Buddhist teachings are written in palm leaf books like this one.

Celebrating Dhamma Day

Dhamma Day is usually celebrated very simply. This is a time to remember the Buddha's first teachings. So, in the temples and monasteries, Buddhist monks and nuns read from Buddhist scriptures and chant the words of the Buddha's first sermon, which is called the First Turning of the Wheel of Truth, or the 'Dhamma Chakra Sutra'. The chanting may last all night.

Many people go to their local temple or monastery to listen to the chanting and to give gifts to the monks and nuns. They may also leave offerings in front of the statues of the Buddha. This is a way of thanking the Buddha for his teachings.

Dhamma Day is also important because it is the beginning of the Rains Retreat.

▼ Celebrating Dhamma Day.

The Rains Retreat

Buddhism began in India and spread first to south east Asia. In ancient times in these places, the yearly rainy season was a time when farmers and many other people had very little work to do. No crops could be planted or harvested during the rains. The rainy season usually lasts for three months.

When Buddhism began, the Buddha and his followers would spend most of their time travelling. Wherever they went they would teach people about Buddhism. But during the rainy season, the Buddha and his followers would spend all of their time in temples and monasteries meditating and studying Buddhism.

Today, the Rains Retreat is a time when Buddhist monks and nuns all over the world remain in their temples, studying and praying.

What happens during the Rains Retreat?

The Rains Retreat begins on the day after Dhamma Day and lasts for three months. For monks and nuns this time is spent in study, meditation and prayer.

However, many ordinary Buddhists who are not monks or nuns also choose to spend part of the Rains Retreat at a monastery, living as a monk or nun for a short time. This is an opportunity for people to learn more about Buddhist teachings, and also a time to worship and meditate.

In some traditions, when a child reaches a certain age, they are sent to a monastery for the Rains Retreat. The children become **NOVICE** monks, or monks in training, for the three months of the Rains Retreat. Their heads are shaved and they live in the same way as the monks and nuns. In the monastery, the children learn all about Buddhism and how to meditate and pray.

Holidays to end the Rains Retreat

The Rains Retreat ends on the Full Moon of October. At the end of the Rains Retreat there may be a holiday to celebrate.

For some families, this is a day to welcome back family members who have spent the Rains Retreat in a monastery. For others, this is a way to share a day of worship with the monks and nuns.

Early in the morning, people begin to arrive at the temple wearing their best clothes. They carry food prepared at home, usually in decorated bowls, and offer it to the monks. After this breakfast, the people are blessed by the monks and many return to their homes. Others choose to remain at the temple and spend the day praying, meditating and listening to the talks.

▼ These boys are spending the Rains Retreat in a monastery as temporary, or novice, monks, learning all about Buddhism. In a few months, they will return to their families.

SCHEDULE for a holiday at the end of the Rains Retreat:

7:00 am	Meditation and morning chanting
10:00 am	Chanting by the monks
10:30 am	Offerings of alms to the monks
11:00 am	Offerings are made to the Buddha
12:00 pm	Lunch
1:00 pm	A talk about Buddhism, in English
1:30 pm	Traditional offering ceremony of money and gifts to the monks and nuns
5:00 pm	Taking the FIVE (OR EIGHT) PRECEPTS: each person agrees to do the following – do not kill, do not steal, always be sexually responsible, do not lie, do not drink alcohol, no entertainment, no soft bed, and no food after midday. Monks agree to do these things at all times, non-monks agree to do the first five at all times.
7:00 pm	A talk about Buddhism, in English
7:30 pm	Meditation
8:00 pm	Evening chanting
8:30 pm	Refreshments

▲ People leave gifts of ALMS money at a temple in England. The money is used to help run the temple or monastery and to pay for charitable works.

In the evening, the monks lead a candle lit procession, making three complete circles around the main temple building. This marks the end of the holiday and of the Rains Retreat.

25

The holy day of Kathina

This holy day is held about one month after the end of the Rains Retreat.

Kathina is also called the Festival of Robes. Buddhist monks and nuns take a vow of poverty, they do not own anything and do not have any money of their own. At the holiday of Kathina, people bring gifts of robes and other items for the monks and nuns to use.

The story of Kathina

When Buddhism began, the Buddha showed the first monks and nuns how to make their own robes. Each monk and nun was expected to cut, sew and dye their own robe. A 'kathin' is a type of loom used for weaving or embroidery.

Celebrating the holiday

People come to the temples and monasteries with gifts of robes, Buddhist literature, kitchen equipment, money, and even building materials. These are all things the monastery and the monks and nuns will need during the year.

◀▲ It is traditional on Kathina to give gifts of new robes and other practical items to the monks and nuns.

The gifts may be handed to the monks and nuns, or placed on a platform and then handed out to individual monks and nuns after a ceremony. After receiving the gifts, the monks and nuns bless each giver.

There may also be a festival or fête at the temple or monastery on this day. This may include traditional food, music and dancing.

Weblink: www.CurriculumVisions.com

Remembering ancestors

In some countries, there are holy days in the Buddhist calendar that remember and honour people's ancestors.

For Buddhists, it is very important to show respect to elders and to remember family members and ancestors who have died.

Most Buddhist traditions have a day or a holy time set aside to remember ancestors. In many Buddhist traditions this holy time is around the 15th day of the seventh Buddhist month (usually June/July). Some Buddhists call this holiday Ullambana. Others call it O-bon, or Ancestor Day.

▼ On Ancestor Day some Buddhists remember the story of Moginlin and how he was told to make offerings to the Buddhist monks for his mother's soul to be released.

One story of Ancestor Day

According to one Buddhist legend, the holiday of Ancestor Day is based on the story of one of Buddha's followers, Moginlin, and his mother.

Moginlin discovers that his mother's spirit is suffering in the land of the dead. So he decides to go to the land of the dead to help her. In the land of the dead, Moginlin finds his mother starving. He offers her food, but when she tries to eat it, the food turns to smouldering pieces of charcoal.

Moginlin went to the Buddha to ask his advice and the Buddha told Moginlin, "In her previous life, your mother insulted the Buddha and the monks. Also, she was greedy and hot-tempered. That is why she is suffering".

Moginlin asked the Buddha if there was any way that he could help his mother. The Buddha told him that he could not help his mother by himself. He told Moginlin to make offerings of five fruits, incense, oil, lamps, candles, and bedding to the Buddhist monks and to pray with them for his mother to be freed from the land of the dead and be reborn.

The Buddha also told Moginlin that by making these offerings, his mother and his other ancestors will escape suffering and attain nirvana (peace). Moginlin did what the Buddha said and his mother was freed from her sufferings.

The day on which Moginlin made the offerings and prayers is celebrated as Ancestor Day.

In some Buddhist traditions, people believe that if we are not good in this life, then we may have to spend time suffering in the 'land of the dead' until we can be reborn into another life. On Ancestor Day the 'Gates of the Dead' are opened and ghosts come back from the land of the dead to visit their loved ones.

So, Ancestor Day is a time when people can help ease the suffering of the ghosts by showing them respect and love, and by leaving them gifts of food, drink and other things.

Celebrating Ullambana

In India, Ancestor Day is called Ullambana. This is a time for people to pray for any family members who have died. It is also a time to show respect to family members who are alive. During the first 14 days of the month, people may visit their older relatives and give them gifts.

▲ Paper flowers with candles in them for celebrating O-bon.

◄ Ancestor Day is a time to visit relatives and to show respect for family members, especially older family members.

▲ In Japan, people celebrate O-bon by floating paper lanterns shaped like flowers in rivers and streams. The candles are a reminder of the spirits of their ancestors.

On Ullambana, people may go to the cemetery and make offerings of prayers, food, water, candles and incense to their departed ancestors.

Many people also go to the temple on this day. In the temple they also make offerings and pray for their ancestors. They also make offerings of food, clothing and other items to the monks and nuns.

Celebrating in Japan

In Japan, Ancestor Day is called O-bon and is a very popular holiday. It is celebrated for four days. O-bon is an important family gathering time, and many people return to their hometowns during the holiday.

On the first day, people clean their houses and place offerings of food and incense on small altars in their houses. Small paper lanterns are hung outside houses to guide the spirits of their ancestors

home. People also visit their family graves to call their ancestors' spirits back home.

During the holiday, traditional dances are held at neighbourhood temples and parks.

On the last night, people send off their ancestors' spirits by placing a candle inside a paper lantern and floating the lantern down a river or stream. There may also be fireworks.

Celebrating in China

In China and Taiwan, Ullambana is also called the Ghost festival, or Chung Yuan Putu. The holiday is celebrated on the 15th day of the seventh month in the Buddhist calendar.

Families make offerings of food and wine to the spirits of their ancestors. They may also burn paper money in small fires as an offering.

Index

Curriculum Visions

Curriculum Visions is a registered trademark of Atlantic Europe Publishing Company Ltd.

Atlantic Europe Publishing

First published in 2007 by
Atlantic Europe Publishing Company Ltd
Copyright © 2007 Earthscape

The right of Lisa Magloff to be identified as the author of this work has been asserted by her in accordance with the Copyright, Designs and Patents Act 1988.

All rights reserved. No part of this publication may be reproduced, stored in a retrieval system, or transmitted in any form or by any means, electronic, mechanical, photocopying, recording or otherwise, without prior permission of the Publisher and the copyright holder.

Author
Lisa Magloff, MA
Religious Adviser
Lama Zangmo, Kagyu Samye Dzong, London Tibetan Buddhist Centre.
Senior Designer
Adele Humphries, BA
Acknowledgements
The publishers would like to thank the following for their help and advice:
The Buddhapadipa Temple, Wimbledon, London and Kagyu Samye Dzong, London Tibetan Buddhist Centre, Lambeth, London.
Photographs
The Earthscape Picture Library, except:
(c=centre, t=top, b=bottom, l=left, r=right)
pages 8–9, 16t, 16–17, 17, 18 (inset), 19br, 20, 24–25 *ShutterStock.*
Illustrations
David Woodroffe

Designed and produced by
Earthscape
Printed in China by
WKT Company Ltd
Buddhist holy days
– Curriculum Visions
A CIP record for this book is available from the British Library
ISBN: 978 1 86214 498 9

This product is manufactured from sustainable managed forests. For every tree cut down at least one more is planted.

Dedicated Web Site
There's more about other great Curriculum Visions packs and a wealth of supporting information on world religions and other subjects at our dedicated web site:
www.CurriculumVisions.com